"This series is a tremendous resource for those wanting to study and teach the Bible with an understanding of how the gospel is woven throughout Scripture. Here are gospel-minded pastors and scholars doing gospel business from all the Scriptures. This is a biblical and theological feast preparing God's people to apply the entire Bible to all of life with heart and mind wholly committed to Christ's priorities."

BRYAN CHAPELL, President Emeritus, Covenant Theological Seminary; Senior Pastor, Grace Presbyterian Church, Peoria, Illinois

"Mark Twain may have smiled when he wrote to a friend, 'I didn't have time to write you a short letter, so I wrote you a long letter.' But the truth of Twain's remark remains serious and universal, because well-reasoned, compact writing requires extra time and extra hard work. And this is what we have in the Crossway Bible study series *Knowing the Bible*. The skilled authors and notable editors provide the contours of each book of the Bible as well as the grand theological themes that bind them together as one Book. Here, in a 12-week format, are carefully wrought studies that will ignite the mind and the heart."

R. KENT HUGHES, Visiting Professor of Practical Theology, Westminster Theological Seminary

"*Knowing the Bible* brings together a gifted team of Bible teachers to produce a high-quality series of study guides. The coordinated focus of these materials is unique: biblical content, provocative questions, systematic theology, practical application, and the gospel story of God's grace presented all the way through Scripture."

PHILIP G. RYKEN, President, Wheaton College

"These *Knowing the Bible* volumes provide a significant and very welcome variation on the general run of inductive Bible studies. This series provides substantial instruction, as well as teaching through the very questions that are asked. *Knowing the Bible* then goes even further by showing how any given text links with the gospel, the whole Bible, and the formation of theology. I heartily endorse this orientation of individual books to the whole Bible and the gospel, and I applaud the demonstration that sound theology was not something invented later by Christians, but is right there in the pages of Scripture."

GRAEME L. GOLDSWORTHY, former lecturer, Moore Theological College; author, *According to Plan*, *Gospel and Kingdom*, *The Gospel in Revelation*, and *Gospel and Wisdom*

"What a gift to earnest, Bible-loving, Bible-searching believers! The organization and structure of the Bible study format presented through the *Knowing the Bible* series is so well conceived. Students of the Word are led to understand the content of passages through perceptive, guided questions, and they are given rich insights and application all along the way in the brief but illuminating sections that conclude each study. What potential growth in depth and breadth of understanding these studies offer! One can only pray that vast numbers of believers will discover more of God and the beauty of his Word through these rich studies."

BRUCE A. WARE, Professor of Christian Theology, The Southern Baptist Theological Seminary

KNOWING THE BIBLE

J. I. Packer, Theological Editor
Dane C. Ortlund, Series Editor
Lane T. Dennis, Executive Editor

• • • • • •

Genesis	Psalms	Jonah, Micah, and Nahum	Ephesians
Exodus	Proverbs		Philippians
Leviticus	Ecclesiastes	Haggai, Zechariah, and Malachi	Colossians and Philemon
Numbers	Song of Solomon		
Deuteronomy	Isaiah	Matthew	1–2 Thessalonians
Joshua	Jeremiah	Mark	1–2 Timothy and Titus
Judges	Lamentations, Habakkuk, and Zephaniah	Luke	
Ruth and Esther		John	Hebrews
1–2 Samuel	Ezekiel	Acts	James
1–2 Kings	Daniel	Romans	1–2 Peter and Jude
1–2 Chronicles	Hosea	1 Corinthians	1–3 John
Ezra and Nehemiah	Joel, Amos, and Obadiah	2 Corinthians	Revelation
Job		Galatians	

• • • • • •

J. I. PACKER is the former Board of Governors' Professor of Theology at Regent College (Vancouver, BC). Dr. Packer earned his DPhil at the University of Oxford. He is known and loved worldwide as the author of the best-selling book *Knowing God*, as well as many other titles on theology and the Christian life. He serves as the General Editor of the ESV Bible and as the Theological Editor for the *ESV Study Bible*.

LANE T. DENNIS is CEO of Crossway, a not-for-profit publishing ministry. Dr. Dennis earned his PhD from Northwestern University. He is Chair of the ESV Bible Translation Oversight Committee and Executive Editor of the *ESV Study Bible*.

DANE C. ORTLUND is Chief Publishing Officer at Crossway. He is a graduate of Covenant Theological Seminary (MDiv, ThM) and Wheaton College (BA, PhD). Dr. Ortlund has authored several books and scholarly articles in the areas of Bible, theology, and Christian living.

1–2 PETER AND JUDE

A 12-WEEK STUDY

Jonathan K. Dodson

CROSSWAY®

WHEATON, ILLINOIS

Knowing the Bible: 1–2 Peter and Jude, A 12-Week Study

Copyright © 2017 by Crossway

Published by Crossway
       1300 Crescent Street
       Wheaton, Illinois 60187

Some content used in this study guide has been adapted from the *ESV Study Bible*, copyright 2008 by Crossway, pages 2401–2423 and 2447–2452. Used by permission. All rights reserved.

Cover design: Simplicated Studio

First printing 2017

Printed in the United States of America

All emphases in Scripture quotations have been added by the author.

Trade paperback ISBN: 978-1-4335-5441-4
PDF ISBN: 978-1-4335-5442-1
Mobipocket ISBN: 978-1-4335-5443-8
EPub ISBN: 978-1-4335-5444-5

Crossway is a publishing ministry of Good News Publishers.

VP		30	29	28	27	26	25	24	23	22	21	20
14	13	12	11	10	9	8	7	6	5	4	3	2

TABLE OF CONTENTS

SERIES PREFACE

KNOWING THE BIBLE, as the series title indicates, was created to help readers know and understand the meaning, the message, and the God of the Bible. Each volume in the series consists of 12 units that progressively take the reader through a clear, concise study of that book of the Bible. In this way, any given volume can fruitfully be used in a 12-week format either in group study, such as in a church-based context, or in individual study. Of course, these 12 studies could be completed in fewer or more than 12 weeks, as convenient, depending on the context in which they are used.

Each study unit gives an overview of the text at hand before digging into it with a series of questions for reflection or discussion. The unit then concludes by highlighting the gospel of grace in each passage ("Gospel Glimpses"), identifying whole-Bible themes that occur in the passage ("Whole-Bible Connections"), and pinpointing Christian doctrines that are affirmed in the passage ("Theological Soundings").

The final component to each unit is a section for reflecting on personal and practical implications from the passage at hand. The layout provides space for recording responses to the questions proposed, and we think readers need to do this to get the full benefit of the exercise. The series also includes definitions of key words. These definitions are indicated by a note number in the text and are found at the end of each chapter.

Lastly, to help understand the Bible in this deeper way, we urge readers to use the ESV Bible and the *ESV Study Bible*, which are available in various print and digital formats, including online editions at esv.org. The Knowing the Bible series is also available online.

May the Lord greatly bless your study as you seek to know him through knowing his Word.

J. I. Packer
Lane T. Dennis

WEEK 1: OVERVIEW

▲

When global unrest, cultural turbulence, personal suffering, destructive theology, or everyday turmoil strikes, how do you respond? It is easy to become overwhelmed by such things, but Peter desires his audience to know that they have a unique ability to step back from their historical situation and view life from a transcendent perspective. In Christ, we possess the gift of gospel optimism. Gospel optimism insists that, no matter how dark the times, we have every reason to hope in Christ.

In the letters of Peter we find no mere spiritual suggestions but divine truths, warnings, and commands meant to give hope. He writes not to a loose collection of spiritually minded individuals but to "a royal priesthood, a holy nation" (1 Pet. 2:9), a living temple created to beam its collective, glorious hope into darkened surroundings. Peter identifies his audience as exiles[1] who, in their various sufferings, possess the hope of Jesus' return, which is to motivate faithful living in the present.

Peter exhorts the exiles to aim not for cultural relevance or dominance but for faithfulness to Jesus. He reminds his readers that gospel hope produces an enduring optimism that shines through issues of personal holiness, attitudes toward authority, interpersonal ethics, and perseverance in suffering. Second Peter and Jude tighten the screws on deceitful teachers and their doctrines while lifting up the truth of God's Word. They anticipate the return of Christ as a time of great judgment and salvation. Amid these heavy themes, Peter and

Jude repeatedly remind their readers that their only hope rests in Jesus' promised return, which will one day bring us, and all creation, into the full glory we can only taste now. Until Jesus' return, the church is to live together as chosen pilgrims, loving one another and contending for the truth as a distinct witness to the glory of God in the risen Christ.

Placing 1–2 Peter and Jude in the Larger Story

With Jesus' birth, life, death, resurrection, and ascension the church has been launched into the world. Starting in Jerusalem and spreading around the world, the church encounters opposition, misunderstanding, and persecution. Writing to Christians scattered throughout modern-day Turkey, Peter calls the early Christians "exiles." This term probably has a double meaning, one theological and one cultural. With the remnant of Israel exiled in Babylon in the background, Peter envisions the church as God's true Israel, exiled in the world. However, as a community of those who are spiritually foreign and socially marginalized, the church is also a community of exiles within their own culture. Jude also picks up on this theme, reminding the church that their identity is in "Jesus, who saved a people out of the land of Egypt" (Jude 5). He exhorts the church to live as saints delivered from sin by Jesus and urges them not to fall into unbelief. The whole church can thus be viewed as a community of exiles—God's chosen and redeemed people called to live for Jesus in this world.

Key Passage

"After you have suffered a little while, the God of all grace, who has called you to his eternal glory in Christ, will himself restore, confirm, strengthen, and establish you. To him be the dominion forever and ever. Amen." (1 Pet. 5:10–11)

Date and Historical Background

First Peter was probably written in the mid-60s AD to Christians scattered throughout "Pontus, Galatia, Cappadocia, Asia, and Bithynia" (1 Pet. 1:1), all areas in modern-day Turkey. Second Peter was likely written closer to the end of Peter's life, in the late 60s. The apostle himself comments that "I know that the putting off of my body will be soon" (2 Pet. 1:14). We are not certain how Peter knew he would soon die. Perhaps this knowledge was an insight from the Holy Spirit, an awareness of intensifying plots to kill him, or a combination of both. Much less is known about Jude, who was probably a brother of James (author of the letter bearing that name) and of Jesus (Gal. 1:19). It is likely that Jude was written before 2 Peter, although various scholars date the letter anywhere between AD 50 and 90. It is clear that Jude has a firm grasp on the Old Testament Scriptures as well as on the gospel of Jesus. He uses this understanding, together with his earnest faith, to respond to the particular issues of false teaching and ungodliness, which pervert the grace of God. He is intent on helping the church "contend for the faith that was once for all delivered to the saints" (Jude 3).

Outline of 1 Peter

I. Hope that Lives into Holiness (1:1–2:3)

    A. Salutation (1:1–2)
    B. A living hope (1:3–12)
    C. Holy together (1:13–2:3)

II. Community Made on the Cornerstone (2:4–12)

III. The Church that Affirms Authority (2:13–3:7)

    A. Submitting to governing authorities (2:13–17)
    B. Submitting in suffering (2:18–25)
    C. Submitting to husbands and honoring wives (3:1–7)

IV. Suffering Together (3:8–4:19)

    A. Community life as witness (3:8–22)
    B. Ceasing from sin (4:1–11)
    C. Suffering well (4:12–19)

V. Humble Together (5:1–14)

    A. Elders and the church (5:1–5a)
    B. Resisting the Devil (5:5b–11)
    C. Closing greetings (5:12–14)

As You Get Started

These three letters apply the hope of Christ to global unrest, cultural turbulence, personal suffering, destructive teachings, and everyday turmoil. Do any such conflicts affect your life? Reflect on your own situation and how you think the books of this study (1–2 Peter, Jude) should challenge you.

What themes catch your attention in these letters? Do any particular passages from 1–2 Peter or Jude come to mind?

How do these letters clarify our understanding of sinful patterns, suffering, salvation, the Christian relationship with society, the end times, or other doctrines?

There are some strange and difficult texts in 1–2 Peter and Jude. Do you find any of them confusing? Are there any specific questions you hope to have answered through this study?

As You Finish This Unit . . .

Pause and ask the Holy Spirit to give you biblical insight, self-understanding, and grace to respond to Christ however he wants you to as you study these letters.

Definition

[1] **Exile** – The term "exile" includes three strands of meaning: (1) physical displacement from home; (2) persecution by society, resulting in suffering; (3) cultural marginalization. To be an exile is to be at home in Christ while foreign to aspects of this world.

Week 2: Hope That Lives into Holiness

1 Peter 1:1–2:3

The Place of the Passage

Peter opens his first letter by identifying himself as an "apostle" (meaning "one who is sent") and his recipients as "exiles." He immediately lifts their spirits with a focus on the electing[1] grace of the Trinity.[2] Then he proceeds to reflect on the hope that springs from being "born again," on our inheritance in Christ, and on the relevance of such things for facing trials and pursuing holiness.

The Big Picture

First Peter 1:1–2:3 inspires us with the truth that what we believe about the future return of Christ ought to have a profound effect on us in the present.

Elect Exiles 11

Reflection and Discussion

Read through the complete passage for this study, 1 Peter 1:1–2:3. Then review the questions below concerning this introductory section to 1 Peter and write your notes on them. (For further background, see the *ESV Study Bible*, pages 2401–2404; available online at esv.org.)

1. Greeting (1:1–2)

Read 1 Peter 2:9–12; 5:12–14 and consider how these texts fill out what Peter means by describing his readers as "exiles." Why would this identification be meaningful to Peter's audience? Is it meaningful to you?

Peter opens his letter with a rich Trinitarian formulation (1:2). What role does each member of the Trinity (Father, Son, and Holy Spirit) play in this verse? How does their work convey grace and peace? How does it give hope?

2. Hope in Suffering (1:3–12)

All three persons of the Trinity collaborate so that we may be born again into a hope that is alive. Why do we need a new birth? According to verses 3 and 23, how do we obtain this new birth?

Notice that we do not *hope* our way into a new life; rather, the gift of new life flowers into hope. To what does that hope point? According to verses 6–9, how should Christ's future work impact us in our present suffering?

We often view suffering as an impediment to joy, but Peter insists that trials can result in "inexpressible" joy. How is that possible? Peter compares suffering to the smelting of metallic ore. How does this metaphor help us understand how to rejoice in hard times?

According to verses 10–12, Old Testament saints anticipated the sufferings and glories of Christ. Can you think of any examples of such saints? How do we benefit from these saints' anticipation? Why do you think angels marvel as they observe redemptive history?

3. Holy Together (1:13–2:3)

Verse 13 begins with "therefore," indicating that everything that precedes this verse is the basis for what Peter will say next. Summarize the basis for Peter's command in this verse and consider how it impacts our call to holiness in verse 15.

How do 1:18–22 and 2:3 show us that holiness involves not just getting far from sin but also must include getting close to God? How might this insight tweak your approach to holiness?

In what ways is holiness a communal endeavor? In which of these ways do you need to grow? What steps can you take to do so?

Verses 22–25 circle back to the theme of the new birth. Although verse 22 may sound like self-purification, "obedience to the truth" must begin with our response to the gospel (Rom. 1:5; 16:26). According to this passage, what does the new birth inevitably produce? How can you take steps to love sincerely (1 Pet. 1:22)?

Read through the following three sections on *Gospel Glimpses*, *Whole-Bible Connections*, and *Theological Soundings*. Then take time to consider the *Personal Implications* these sections may have for you.

Gospel Glimpses

ATONEMENT. The notion of being sprinkled with blood, and the sacrifices required to produce such blood, can sound archaic or crude to modern ears. Yet the Bible frequently mentions the manipulation of blood sacrifices in order to make atonement. The term *atonement*, which expresses the thought of "making at one," refers to bringing two estranged parties together. Atonement law in Exodus 24 required the death of an unblemished, spotless, "perfect" animal to bring God and man back together. In this ritual, the person was sprinkled with the blood of the perfect sacrifice. Why? Because the reason for the estrangement, the crime, had to be dealt with, or "atoned" for. The death of the sacrifice was a substitute for the punishment and death of the sinner. These sacrifices pointed forward to Jesus, who died the death we deserved and sprinkled us with the proof that we do not have to die. This is a deep grace that brings two estranged parties, God and man, back together so that we can live "at one" with God. In this profound display of mercy, we receive grace while God receives glory.

BORN AGAIN. Atonement makes new birth possible. Spiritual rebirth, or being born again, can also sound strange, but the intrusion of light into darkness can be a little disorienting. Peter uses the imagery of spiritual rebirth to communicate the necessity and hope of being born again (1 Pet. 1:3, 23; 2:2). Jesus explained that no one can enter the kingdom of God unless they are born again (John 3:3). With new birth comes new life: the power to live a truly human life, to turn from sin, and to enjoy God's love and grace. Apart from the new birth, we distort our humanity through self-centered living. The beauty of the new birth is that we do nothing to gain this new life. No one chooses to be born; rather, God chooses to give us new life! Salvation in Christ is a gift that is applied and enjoyed through the Holy Spirit (Titus 3:4–5), who enables us to revel in life with God.

Whole-Bible Connections

TRUE INHERITANCE. Peter declares that the object of our hope is "an inheritance that is imperishable, undefiled, and unfading, kept in heaven for you" (1 Pet. 1:4). What is this inheritance? This word is used in the Old Testament to refer to the land promised to Israel, a land flowing with milk and honey, where God himself would dwell with his people (Gen. 15:7; Deut. 1:8; Josh. 13:6). In the New Testament, this land is expanded to include the whole world (Gal. 3:18; Rom. 4:13; see also Heb. 11:8–10). The inherited world is described by Peter as imperishable; like the resurrection body, this is a world that will never break down. Peter is pointing our hope toward a world where decay has no sway, corruption never enters in, and nothing ever wears out. Our inheritance is a sinless, resurrected existence in God's renewed heavens and earth (2 Pet. 3:13).

Theological Soundings

HOPE. Sometimes hope is thought of as an event: the revelation of Jesus Christ (1 Pet. 1:7, 13), the day of visitation (2:12), the revelation of his glory (4:13) and ours (5:1, 4), the ultimate display of eternal glory, dominion, and power (5:10–11). At other times this hope is thought of as an age: the last time (1:5), which is from heaven (1:4) and is manifested in these last times (1:20), when the end of all things is at hand (4:7). The Gospels refer to this age as the "kingdom" of God, which has broken into this world but has not been fully manifested. Our hope, then, cannot be in this world but is in events that reveal the future world and her Savior and King. So, while Peter expresses hope sometimes as an event and other times as an age, it is always ultimately centered in a person—in the person, work, and return of Jesus Christ, who will display his glory in all things. This hope should cause us to hold possessions and sufferings more loosely, and to hold Christ and his inheritance more tightly.

HOLINESS. Often we think of holiness as a scale, with God at the top. We then rank ourselves somewhere on that scale. But God is not at the top; he is the very measure of holiness itself. He is referred to in Scripture as "holy, holy, holy," a Hebrew expression conveying the idea of perfect holiness (Isa. 6:3; Rev. 4:8). God is wholly and totally other, transcendent and incomparable. This means that "holy" is not one attribute among others, such as love, omnipotence, or wisdom. Rather, all of God's attributes define what those terms truly mean: true love is the holy love of God; true power is his holy power; and so on, all beyond scrutiny. Because God *is* pure holiness, he is therefore a perfect judge of what is imperfect or unholy. This should generate reverence for God, since "all have sinned and fall short of the glory of God" (Rom. 3:23). Yet God tells his people to be holy. Holiness for us, then, is not merely getting away from sin but also must include getting close to God, who is the very definition of holiness. This is impossible unless such holiness comes to us, as it does in a spotless Lamb, slain on the cross to absorb our sin and draw us close to God. Drawn close to God by the loving sacrifice of his Son, we are compelled to make decisions that continually draw us closer to him and reflect his holy character.

Personal Implications

Take time to reflect on the implications of 1 Peter 1:1–2:3 for your own life. Consider what you have learned that might lead you to praise God, repent of sin, and trust in his promises. You can make notes below on the personal implications of the (1) *Gospel Glimpses*, (2) *Whole-Bible Connections*, (3) *Theological Soundings*, and (4) the passage as a whole.

1. Gospel Glimpses

2. Whole-Bible Connections

3. Theological Soundings

4. 1 Peter 1:1–2:3

▶ **As You Finish This Unit . . .**

Look back through this unit to reflect on some key things the Lord is teaching you. Respond to him in prayer.

Definitions

[1] **Election** – God's sovereign appointment of people to faith in Jesus Christ for salvation and a place in his body, the church. Jesus calls these people the "elect" (Matt. 24:22, 24, 31). This doctrine has wide-ranging support in Scripture (John 10; Romans 8–9; Ephesians 1; 2 Peter 1) and frequently appears in the OT in language describing those who are "called" or "chosen" (Deut. 7:6–7; Ex. 19:4–6).

[2] **Trinity** – The Godhead as it exists in three distinct persons: Father, Son, and Holy Spirit. There is one God, yet he is three persons; there are not three Gods, nor do the three persons merely represent different aspects or modes of a single God. While the term Trinity is not found in the Bible, the concept is repeatedly assumed and affirmed by the writers of Scripture (Gen. 1:26; Matt. 28:19; Gal. 4:6; 2 Thess. 2:13–14; Heb. 10:29).

WEEK 3: COMMUNITY FOUNDED ON THE CORNERSTONE

1 Peter 2:4–12

▲

After establishing a profound basis for Christian hope no matter how hard the times, Peter next draws attention to the implications of our hope for our life within a community of fellow believers. Observing the need to *taste* the Lord in order to grow up into salvation (1 Pet. 2:1–3), Peter zeroes in on the centrality of Christ and the importance of community. He locates the church within the rich history of Israel by describing the people of God as a grand temple of living stones fitted together by the unique presence of Christ, the cornerstone.

The Big Picture

This passage demonstrates that Christianity is not a private religion but a public community united in Christ.

Reflection and Discussion

Read through the entire text for this study, 1 Peter 2:4–12. Then interact with the following questions concerning this section of 1 Peter and record your notes on them. (For further background, see the *ESV Study Bible*, pages 2407–2408; available online at esv.org.)

Peter brushes formalistic religion aside by focusing our hope on a person: "As you come to him, a living stone rejected by men but in the sight of God chosen and precious . . ." (v. 4). Are you ever tempted to do the opposite, sliding into formalistic religion instead of pursuing a Christ-centered faith?

Peter piles up Old Testament texts that describe the cornerstone of a great building. What is unique about this cornerstone? How should its unique qualities impact the way you relate to God and to your own faith community?

In verse 9, Peter rattles off a list of communal descriptors of the church. Make a list of these descriptors and briefly note how each one challenges or affirms your practice of community. Ask the Spirit to search your heart and give you greater conviction about being a part of God's "royal priesthood."

According to verse 9, why do God's people exist? How can you and your faith community "proclaim the excellencies" of God in your own mission field? What "dark-to-light" changes are occurring in your heart and life that you could share with your neighbors or coworkers?

In verse 11, Peter returns to the exile theme. What marks the exile here? Do you view holiness as something mandatory or as merely optional? According to verse 12, why should you keep your conduct "honorable"?

Read through the following three sections on *Gospel Glimpses*, *Whole-Bible Connections*, and *Theological Soundings*. Then take time to consider the *Personal Implications* these sections may have for you.

Gospel Glimpses

CORNERSTONE. The concept of the cornerstone has a rich and varied background in the Old Testament. Such a stone may have been the first stone set at the corner of a building, determining the direction of all the rest of its stones; or it may have been the stone placed at the top of an arch to hold it together. Psalm 118:22 describes one such stone that was rejected as unsuitable by the builders of a new temple (see also Isa. 28:16). Zechariah views such a stone as a "top stone" of a new temple (Zech. 4:7). As this cornerstone theology unfolds,

Peter calls it a "living stone." In Acts 4:10–11, he alludes to Psalm 118, connecting the rejected stone to the resurrection of Christ. The stone rejected by men was raised by God to become the foundation of a renewed temple of other living stones. As the living, resurrected stone, Jesus magnetically calls others "stones" to snap into place to form a history-spanning, ethnically diverse temple of living stones. Without the redemptive power of the cornerstone, the cosmic temple cannot exist. But with the cornerstone, Israel is rebuilt around its true Messiah as people flood in, shouting praises to God.

Whole-Bible Connections

TEMPLE. In Isaiah 6, we find a vision of a cosmic temple: God on the throne, with his robe filling the earth, which is his footstool. Seraphim (angelic beings) fill the cosmic court, singing praises to God. Isaiah stands before the great God of the temple, with an altar between them. These features reveal the cosmos to be an archetypal temple, and this temple likeness is replicated wherever God's presence is found. Eden, too, is a temple containing the presence of God, priests who work and guard the garden-temple, and an angel who guards the entrance (Genesis 2–3). When God chooses to dwell among Israel, he gives detailed plans for a temple-like tabernacle. This is followed by the creation of Solomon's temple. Reminiscent of the garden-temple, this temple's walls are carved with images of flowers, trees, gourds, and angels (1 Kings 6). It should come as no surprise, then, that when we reach the New Testament, temple imagery is expanded to include the church, which is where God's spirit dwells and which is made up of believers, whose bodies are mini-temples (1 Cor. 3:17; 6:19; Eph. 2:19–21). These saints are themselves described as priests who offer living sacrifices (1 Pet. 2:5; see also Rom. 12:1).

Theological Soundings

DAY OF VISITATION. According to the Old Testament prophets, God will come to earth at the end of history to judge his enemies and restore his people. This is frequently referred to as the "day of the Lord" (Isa. 13:9; Joel 1–3; Zechariah 12–14; Mal. 4:5). Jeremiah uses the term "time [or "year"] of their visitation" frequently (Jer. 8:12; 10:15; and 11:23 KJV) to refer to the same event (compare Luke 19:44 ESV). God's "visits" may bring blessing (Gen. 21:1; 50:24), and when paired with the glory of God such references often point to salvation (Acts 13:48; Rom 4:20). Perhaps Peter has both judgment and salvation in view when referring to a future "day of visitation" on which believers will "glorify God" (1 Pet. 2:12). Many will come to faith after marveling at the good deeds of the saints, while those who mock the church will be judged.

Personal Implications

Take time to reflect on the implications of 1 Peter 2:4–12 for your own life. Consider what you have learned that might lead you to praise God, repent of sin, and trust in his promises. You can make notes below on the personal implications of the (1) *Gospel Glimpses*, (2) *Whole-Bible Connections*, (3) *Theological Soundings*, and (4) the passage as a whole.

1. Gospel Glimpses

2. Whole-Bible Connections

3. Theological Soundings

4. 1 Peter 2:4–12

As You Finish This Unit . . .

Look back through this unit to reflect on some key things the Lord is teaching you. Respond to him in prayer.

WEEK 4: THE CHURCH THAT AFFIRMS AUTHORITY

1 Peter 2:13–3:7

▲

With hope-filled Christians gathered in a community that bears corporate witness to the gospel, Peter proceeds to explain how the church should relate to authority in different spheres of society. He addresses governmental institutions, economic systems, and marriage. This further reveals the missional orientation of Peter's letter.

The Big Picture

In 1 Peter 2:13–3:7, Peter shows how Christians should relate to authority. He challenges revolutionary and capitulatory extremes by urging Christians to allow their response to be guided by faith, not dictated by circumstances.

Reflection and Discussion

Read through the passage for this study, 1 Peter 2:13–3:7. Then review the questions below concerning proper submission to authority and write your notes on them. (For further background, see the *ESV Study Bible*, pages 2408–2409; available online at esv.org.)

1. Submitting to Governing Authorities (2:13–17)

Since Christianity did not enjoy Rome's legal protection, many were skeptical of the early gospel movement, thinking it seditious and a threat to governing authorities. How does Peter point believers in a different direction? How does your attitude toward your various governing authorities compare?

Read and consider Romans 13:1–7. Do the apostles place any limits on our submission to governing authorities? How should believers respond if such authorities punish those who do good or praise those who do evil?

How would your attitude toward governing authorities change if you took Peter's counsel to heart: "Honor everyone. Love the brotherhood. Fear God. Honor the emperor." (1 Pet. 2:17)? Why should we submit to governing authorities?

2. Submitting in Suffering (2:18–25)

It is surprising to some modern readers that Peter does not repudiate slavery. Instead, he exhorts slaves to submit to their masters, even if such masters treat them cruelly. According to verses 19–20, what benefit is there in honoring authorities even when they are unjust?

Given the false political impressions of Christianity in Peter's day, why might it have been wise for the apostle not to call slaves to revolt?

When we suffer unjustly, it can be tempting to lash out. What alternative example does Jesus provide (vv. 21–23)?

Even if we can escape suffering (and sometimes we can and should), lapsing into vengeance, gossip, murder, yelling, or hatred does not actually enable us to escape. These attempts to cope with unjust circumstances simply injure us and others more. How, then, does Christ's response to suffering provide a better example ?

When Jesus suffered, he showed mercy to his persecutors; however, he did not give up on justice. Instead, "When he suffered, he did not threaten, but continued entrusting himself to him who judges justly" (v. 23). This tells us that mercy and justice can coexist, and that our longing for justice can be entrusted to the just Judge of all. Think about a time when you suffered unjustly. How can you apply these examples of showing mercy and hoping in God for justice to that experience?

Read 1 Peter 2:24–25. How is Jesus not only the example but also the power for enduring unjust suffering?

3. Submitting to Husbands and Honoring Wives (3:1–7)

Submission in marriage is a difficult and often misunderstood topic. What does it bring to mind for you? Read Ephesians 5:15–33. How does this description balance or change your impression of submission?

The submission called for in 1 Peter is unqualified, but this is not because submission comes with no qualifications. Peter's intent is to: (a) address the issue of submission as it pertains to unbelieving spouses and (b) get to the topic of true, inner beauty. Why does he insist on respectful submission to a spouse who does not share our Christian beliefs?

While true submission can lead to a husband's being "won" to Christ, the primary motivation for submission is not evangelism but worship according to the order of creation. Such submission is to be done with a quiet spirit, which "in God's sight is very precious." This is something that a wife does ultimately for God. How does 1 Peter 3:7 show us that submission does not spring from an inequality between men and women?

First Peter 3:3 seems to condemn outer beauty, but it is important to understand the first-century context of this exhortation. The issue is not with *braids* per se but with braids laced with extravagance, i.e., gold and pearls. The key concern is extravagant dress, "costly attire." Extravagant hairdos were promoted by elite, imperial women who laced their braids with wealth to show off their status. Some of the clothing of Peter's day cost upwards of 7,000 denarii, the earning of which would take about 19 years of typical day-labor. These Greco-Roman practices were impacting believers, as church gatherings were becoming a competition in external beauty, and this was distracting attention from God as the focus of worship. Do you encounter similar temptations to measure your beauty in competition with others, rather than in the context of your relationship with Christ?

The Greek word for "adorn" is *kosmeō*, the root of the English word "cosmetic." Peter is commanding believers not to settle for a beauty that is purely cosmetic, on the outside. Instead, we are to seek beauty in the hidden person of the heart. Keeping in mind that a strong woman like Sarah is used as an example, what does it mean to have a gentle and quiet spirit? Sarah was under no illusions regarding Abraham's shortcomings, so why would she call him "lord"? How can married readers apply Sarah's example to their own speech and behavior today?

The exhortation to live with one's wife "in an understanding way" literally translates as "according to knowledge." What are some ways in which a husband's knowledge of God and of the gospel should affect his marriage?

Although Peter uses only one verse to address husbands, the penalty for not honoring their wives seems to be steeper. What is it? Why does he warn husbands of this danger?

Read through the following three sections on *Gospel Glimpses, Whole-Bible Connections*, and *Theological Soundings*. Then take time to consider the *Personal Implications* these sections may have for you.

Gospel Glimpses

BY HIS STRIPES YOU ARE HEALED. First Peter 2:21–25 pieces together passages from Isaiah 53, where the prophet predicts the coming of a suffering servant who would bear our griefs and sorrows, our sins and our transgressions, in order to win us peace with God. In 1 Peter 2:22, the suffering servant commits no sin, nor is deceit found in his mouth; Jesus was innocent and pure, a scorned yet spotless lamb, true to the end. In verse 23 he is reviled but does not revile in return; when Jesus suffered, he "did not threaten, but continued entrusting himself to him who judges justly." In verse 24, we discover why Jesus endured all of this: to bear our sins in his body on the tree, that we might "die to sin and live to righteousness." Jesus was charged with the sin of the world not only so that we might be forgiven and accepted by God, but also so that we might live to righteousness. As if that were not enough, verse 24 tells us that by his wounds we are healed, that his stripes make us whole. Jesus wrought good out of sorrow; God wounded his Son to heal sinners. Out of pain comes joy; out of death comes life. Surely there is no greater beauty, no sweeter message, than that of God dying to heal the world.

SHEPHERD OF YOUR SOULS. Christianity is not a mere religious system; it is a way of relating to and enjoying our Creator as our Redeemer. First Peter 2:21–25 makes this plain. What God requires of us—unjust suffering and righteous living—he himself performs at his own expense. We have an intensely personal God who relates to us as Father, Son, and Holy Spirit. The Son is called "the Shepherd and Overseer of your souls" (v. 25). The word "soul" is often misunderstood as immaterial, but in fact it refers to the whole person (mind, body, spirit). By claiming to be the Shepherd of our souls, Jesus is making a wholehearted investment in our livelihood. He desires for us to flourish in every way, even if it meant, in his case, that he ceased to live for a time. When we were due to hang on the tree, Jesus hung there in our place. Over and over we see poetic glimpses of the gospel in this passage, glimpses into the substitutionary death, sinless life, and unfathomable love of Jesus. With such whole-person interest demonstrated to us, how could we not aim to live righteously for him?

Whole-Bible Connections

TRUE ISRAEL. The New Testament is filled with connections to the Old Testament. This interplay between the Testaments reveals the Bible to be one big story that hinges on Christ. Peter quotes the Old Testament extensively, especially in 2:18–25. In 2:22 he quotes Isaiah 53:9: "He committed no sin, neither was deceit found in his mouth." This citation comes from a chapter that predicts the advent of the Messiah and describes his sufferings in detail. The Messiah's suffering would reconcile Israel with God and make them righteous (Isa. 53:11). Peter draws attention to Jesus' unjust suffering, saying that he "committed no sin." Peter also reveals Jesus to be the one true Israelite. Since Adam, all the patriarchs, prophets, judges, priests, and kings had failed to be true to God's law. Yet there would be one who was true to the end, who never uttered an untrue word, with no deceit found in his mouth. The marvel of the gospel is that Jesus confers that status upon us, who do not deserve it. In John 1:45–47, Jesus meets Nathanael and says, "Behold, an Israelite indeed, in whom there is no deceit!" Jesus deliberately places what has been said about him onto Nathanael. Why? Because Nathanael believes Jesus to be the promised Messiah and the King of Israel, and by faith what is true morally of Jesus becomes true of Nathanael. The one true Israelite remakes Israel into the true people of God, and now people from every nation are forgiven and without deceit!

Theological Soundings

MARRIAGE. The Bible begins and ends with marriage (Gen. 2:18–25; Rev. 19:6–10). Marriage between a woman and a man is a wonderful gift, but it is also something meant to point to something else. Paul describes it as a profound mystery that "refers to Christ and the church" (Eph. 5:32). The warm, relational, loving headship and submission of husband and wife are meant to depict the church's relationship with Christ. We honor him with our respectful obedience while marveling at his loving sacrifice for us. This gives marriage between a woman and a man great dignity and divine purpose.

Personal Implications

Take time to reflect on the implications of 1 Peter 2:13–3:7 for your own life. Consider what you have learned that might lead you to praise God, repent of sin, and trust in his promises. You can make notes below on the personal implications of the (1) *Gospel Glimpses*, (2) *Whole-Bible Connections*, (3) *Theological Soundings*, and (4) the passage as a whole.

1. Gospel Glimpses

2. Whole-Bible Connections

3. Theological Soundings

4. 1 Peter 2:13–3:7

As You Finish This Unit . . .

Look back through this unit to reflect on some key things the Lord is teaching you. Respond to him as if he were in your presence.

Week 5: Suffering Together

1 Peter 3:8–4:19

After addressing different types of people in the church, particularly in relation to authority, Peter discusses how we should behave as a corporate community. Calling us to unity, charity, and humility, he lays the groundwork for our collective witness amid a hostile society.

The Big Picture

In 1 Peter 3:8–4:19 we discover the counterintuitive call not to seek revenge but to bless those who snub and marginalize us, just as Jesus did.

Reflection and Discussion

Read through the complete passage for this study, 1 Peter 3:8–4:19. Then review the questions below concerning this section of 1 Peter and write your notes below. (For further background, see the *ESV Study Bible*, pages 2410–2412; available online at esv.org.)

1. Community Life as Witness (3:8–22)

After addressing submission in the realms of government, vocation, and marriage, Peter insists on the importance of unity within the church. Read Ephesians 4:1–16 and reflect on why church unity is so important. According to Peter, what are four marks of unity? Why would these marks foster greater togetherness? In what ways do you need to grow in these four areas?

In 1 Peter 3:9–12, notice how this radical, familial unity produces people who bless when hurt. Read Genesis 12:1–3 and observe the blessings God promises. What happens when Abraham is blessed by God?

Blessing transfers the favor we receive onto others. Repaying evil for evil, on the other hand, refuses to show favor and insists on keeping score. Can you think of ways this mentality has worked against unity in your relationships? What steps can you take to be more of a blessing?

According to verses 9–12, why should we commit to being a people who bless others, especially when it is hard? How do our interactions within the church affect our witness outside the church?

Verse 15 is often used to justify a rational defense of the gospel that can at times lead to sharp and demeaning comments toward others. How do verses 14–17 challenge that approach, without invalidating the need for a rational defense? List the winsome ways in which we are to give a reason for our hope.

How does the imperative to "honor Christ the Lord as holy" affect the way in which we defend our faith to others, especially those who are hostile?

In verse 18, Peter grounds our winsome suffering in Christ's unique work. What is it about Jesus' work in this verse that motivates winsome suffering together? Why should this lead to blessing others instead of keeping score?

Verses 18–22 have puzzled commentators. How did Christ preach to "spirits in prison"? One popular view is that Jesus descended into hell, where some evildoers from Noah's time were kept, and preached the gospel to them, giving them a second chance at salvation. However, the text refers to "spirits," which when used in the plural is typically reserved for angels. Read Jude 6 to determine who the spirits in prison are.

Now, consider the fact that the word "proclaimed" does not necessarily imply a gospel presentation but can also be used to mean proclaiming something else (Rom. 2:21; Gal. 5:11; Rev. 5:2). In light of 1 Peter 3:22, what might Jesus have proclaimed to the spirits in prison?

The resurrection and ascension of Jesus result in victory over evil and salvation for the repentant. How does the Noah episode symbolize what Christ accomplished? How does baptism mirror this? What gives us a clear conscience before God?

2. Ceasing from Sin (4:1–11)

Peter returns to the theme of Christ's suffering, but this time he considers its implications for holiness. According to 4:1–2, what is the connection between

Christ's suffering and our approach to sin? Read 1 Peter 2:24 to help you understand what Peter means when he says we have "ceased from sin."

Peter exhorts us to arm ourselves with the way of thinking that Christ exemplified. True Christianity requires a militant intentionality to combat the passions of the flesh.[1] Do you need to repent of a passive stance toward sin in general or toward some fleshly behavior in particular? Are you willing to suffer and be ridiculed or "maligned" (v. 4) in order not to sin? Are there sins in this list (v. 3) that you would rather commit than endure ridicule for refusing to participate in?

In verse 6, Peter states that "the gospel was preached even to those who are dead." In light of the phrase "the living and the dead" in verse 5, this probably means people who heard the gospel while they were living but who are now dead. How should the fact that our deceased Christian friends heard and believed the gospel affect our own perseverance amid suffering and persecution? (In answering this question, consider the last few words of the verse.)

When Peter says, "The end of all things is at hand" (v. 7), he puts the Christian life in the context of all of world history. Read 1 Peter 1:5, 10–11 to discern what Peter is referring to as "the end." With 4:8–11 in view, list the ways that living in the "end times"[2] should affect the community life of the local church.

3. How to Suffer Well (4:12–19)

In this passage, Peter resumes from chapter 1 the theme of rejoicing in suffering. Why is to "share Christ's sufferings" (v. 13) something to rejoice in? When we are suffering, things can be confusing, but on the other side of suffering we gain greater perspective. With that in mind, consider why Peter says that joy will increase when Christ's glory is revealed.

In verse 15, Peter contrasts sharing in Christ's suffering with suffering as the result of sin. This warning comes with the threat of judgment. The idea of judgment is not popular today, but without it society would be in utter chaos. All will be judged, the living and the dead (4:17). How should God's threat of judgment affect how you suffer?

Romans 6:23 reminds us that we all deserve death, yet Jesus bore death in order to extend eternal life to us. How should God's promise of salvation motivate you amid suffering? How does 1 Peter 4:19 offer you hope for justice amid your sorrow?

_____

_____

_____

_____

_____

_____

Read through the following three sections on *Gospel Glimpses*, *Whole-Bible Connections*, and *Theological Soundings*. Then take time to consider the *Personal Implications* these sections may have for you.

Gospel Glimpses

ONCE FOR SINS TO BRING US TO GOD. First Peter 3:18 says, "Jesus suffered once for sins, the righteous for the unrighteous, that he might bring us to God." When Peter says that Jesus suffered once, he is surveying the whole of Jesus' suffering for mankind, culminating in his crucifixion and death. Jesus' suffering stands as a unique, unrepeatable, all-powerful act. Because of this, we do not have to suffer in order to receive God's favor, earn his forgiveness, or enjoy his love. The penalty owed for our sinful rebellion was fully and finally paid by Jesus on the cross. However, this was not merely a spiritual transaction. The text tells us that its purpose was to bring us to God. The word "bring" means "bring into the presence of." When a leper was removed from Israel's camp so as not to contaminate the community, he had to be inspected for healing before returning to the community and its worship. The leper was "brought into the presence" of the priest for approval and readmission. Similarly, Jesus' mediatorial work brings us into the personal presence of God, whole, healed, and fully admitted into the fellowship of the Trinity.

COST OF DISCIPLESHIP. Throughout this passage Peter challenges us to follow Jesus even when it causes us to face ridicule and scorn. He asks us to be willing to suffer rather than sin. Peter knew there was a cost to following Jesus. If we are unwilling to lose a friend for following Christ, we are following our friend, not Christ. When we follow sinful passions, we act as though Christ had not made us dead to sin and alive to God. As a result, our sense of self gets bigger while God grows smaller. Sacrifice becomes undesirable and we drift further and further from Jesus. This cheapens grace. What the world needs today is not more intelligent or more gifted people but more *unimportant* people, ordinary people who are completely "taken" with an extraordinary Christ. The world desperately needs those who are willing to follow Jesus, no matter the cost, so that others can see what they have seen—the God to whom belongs glory and dominion forever and ever. This is costly discipleship in light of precious grace.

Whole-Bible Connections

THE SPIRIT OF GLORY. The Holy Spirit appears early in the pages of Scripture, hovering over the waters of the deep (Gen. 1:2) to create the cosmos. This hovering image alludes to the movement of a bird's wings. Together with the Father and the Son, the Spirit makes man and woman in God's image and commissions them to be fruitful and multiply, to rule and subdue the earth (Gen. 1:28–30). The Spirit leads Israel out of Egypt and through the wilderness in a pillar of cloud by day and fire by night. As the work of the Spirit unfolds over time, he visits and empowers Old Testament characters; however, it is not until Jesus' death and resurrection that he enters and creates a new Israel. At Pentecost (Acts 2), the early church is filled with the Holy Spirit, and the rushing sound reappears, together with fire reminiscent of the pillar of cloud and fire that led Israel through the wilderness. The Spirit is God's pledge to go with the church and empower us to trust Jesus, to spread the gospel, and to glorify God through creative endeavors. This is the "Spirit of glory" that rests on us (1 Pet. 4:14).

Theological Soundings

ASCENSION. Why send the best proof of the Christian story packing to heaven? To answer this, we need to consider what Jesus is doing in heaven at the right hand of God. *One reason for the ascension is that salvation is not complete until Jesus stands before God.* We need a legal representative to stand before a holy God and say, "They are forgiven, acquitted, and righteous." If the lawyer leaves, we have no representation. The author of Hebrews writes that Jesus "is able to save completely those who draw near to God through him, since he always lives to make intercession for them" (Heb. 7:25 ESV footnote). Jesus stands before our just Judge, triumphantly pleading our case. *Second, salvation is not complete until someone overthrows the powers of evil.* What good is it to be forgiven, even to possess a righteous status, only to struggle forever with sin in a broken world? When Jesus ascends to God's right hand, he signals the overthrow of sin and evil; he puts sin and evil on notice. He deposes the powers with a promise to return and banish sin, death, and evil.

Personal Implications

Take time to reflect on the implications of 1 Peter 3:8–4:19 for your own life today. Consider what you have learned that might lead you to praise God, repent of sin, and trust in his promises. You can make notes below on the personal implications of the (1) *Gospel Glimpses*, (2) *Whole-Bible Connections*, (3) *Theological Soundings*, and (4) the passage as a whole.

1. Gospel Glimpses

2. Whole-Bible Connections

3. Theological Soundings

4. 1 Peter 3:8–4:19

As You Finish This Unit . . .

Look back through this unit to reflect on some key things the Lord is teaching you. Respond to him as if he were in your presence—as in fact he is!

Definitions

[1] **Flesh** – In Scripture this is a metaphor for sinful living based on unbelief in God and his promises. When using this metaphor, the writers of the NT do not intend to belittle or devalue the body. After all, Jesus took on flesh and rose from the dead in physical form. When, therefore, Paul tells us to "put to death" the things of the flesh (e.g., Rom. 8:13; Col. 3:5), he is referring not to the physical body but to the sinful habits and beliefs associated with our pre-Christian identity.

[2] **End times** – The period of time beginning with Christ's first coming and extending to his return (Heb. 1:2; Acts 2:17; Matt. 24:4–9; Dan. 12:1–3).

WEEK 6: HUMBLE TOGETHER

1 Peter 5:1–14

The Place of the Passage

Having addressed the prominent themes of suffering, holiness, submission to authority, and community life, Peter reminds the scattered exiles that all of these issues are to be worked out within the church. Beginning with the elders, he exhorts the people of God to humble themselves under God and toward one another. A humble, interdependent community is the chief witness of these truths to the world. Perseverance in this pursuit is a collective endeavor. Then comes the reward of our calling, a plunge into eternal glory—life full of grace, in a renewed cosmos, under the perfect rule of God—where grace and peace will flow forever.

The Big Picture

In 1 Peter 5:1–14, Peter focuses on the important relationship between elders and the church and on the essential ingredient of humility in order to pursue all that he has addressed in this letter.

> ## Reflection and Discussion

Read through 1 Peter 5:1–14, the focus of this week's study. Following this, review the questions below concerning this section of 1 Peter and write your responses to them. (For further background, see the *ESV Study Bible*, pages 2412–2413; available online at esv.org.)

1. Elders and the Church (5:1–5a)

Why does Peter preface his exhortation to elders by commenting on what he has witnessed and what he will partake of (5:1)? How should this influence the way we read his words?

In verse 2 Peter ascribes spiritual authority to the elders of the local church. In light of verses 3b–4, where does this authority come from? Read 1 Timothy 5:17–20 alongside 1 Peter 5:5–6. How should the church support their elders? What is one way you could express support for your elders?

How should elder authority be exercised? Can you think of ways elders might domineer or lead for "shameful gain" today? According to 1 Timothy 5:1, 19–20, how should we respond to elders who misuse authority? In light of their weighty responsibilities, pause to pray for your elders.

Read 1 Peter 5:5–6. Why is humility such an important ingredient in order for the church to thrive? Notice the direction of grace. Which way does it flow? How are we able to be recipients of God's grace?

Considering the inheritance of 1 Peter 1:3–9 and the promises in 5:10, what does being "[exalted] at the proper time" mean?

What is the relationship between anxiety and humility in verses 6–7? Why do you think proud people tend to be more anxious than humble people?

2. Resisting the Devil (5:5b–11)

Verse 8 reminds us that we have a great foe in our Christian life. The word for "devil"[1] means adversary, and he is depicted as a ravenous lion. Do you take this adversary seriously? List the various ways in which we can oppose the Devil, and reflect on how you can better practice these strategies.

How do verses 10–11 inspire confidence in our battle against sin, temptation, and the Devil? Read James 4:7 and notice the power we have in Christ to overcome the Devil. Be encouraged that the "lion" is on a leash and the Savior is coming back!

3. Final Greetings (5:12–14)

Peter closes out his letter by pointing not to himself but to Silvanus. What does he have to say about Silvanus, and how does this underscore themes in the book? In light of all you have learned, what should faithfulness look like in your daily life?

Peter refers to his whole letter as "the true grace of God." How would you treat the Bible if you really viewed Scripture in this way? According to verse 12, how are we to respond to the true grace of God?

The reference to "Babylon" in verse 13 is a cryptic reference to Rome and a reminder that we are exiles. What words or ideas does Peter reproduce from his opening in this closing of the letter?

Reflect on Peter's opening prayer, "grace and peace be multiplied to you." How has God done this for you throughout this letter? What role has Jesus played in accomplishing this? Pause to praise him, together with the Father and the Spirit, for how God has ministered to you.

Read through the following three sections on *Gospel Glimpses*, *Whole-Bible Connections*, and *Theological Soundings*. Then take time to consider the *Personal Implications* these sections may have for you.

Gospel Glimpses

CROWN OF GLORY. Peter writes, "When the chief Shepherd appears, you will receive the unfading crown of glory" (5:4). A crown is something bestowed to reflect status. It is typically reserved for a king, but Jesus promises to share his status (see Heb. 2:9) with us, representing our new status in him. We are called "fellow heirs" with Christ (Rom. 8:17) and will be permitted to enter his courts with thanksgiving and praise. We are crowned with his affection and given royal status as his sons and daughters. How is this possible? Jesus fought through sin and death to emerge with glorious resurrection life. As the Lord of life, he grants his crown to those who persevere: "Be faithful unto death, and I will give you the crown of life" (Rev. 2:10; see also James 1:12). The crown promised to us is a symbol of the new status, new life, and utter glory bestowed on us by King Jesus. When we see him, we will cast our crowns at his feet in total adoration and praise.

GRACE. When asked what set Christianity apart from all other religions, C. S. Lewis replied, "That's easy; it's grace." Generally speaking, grace is receiving what we do not deserve. Standing next to a glorious, holy, and just God, all men deserve death and hell. To be sure, there are many common graces that all humans enjoy (Matt. 5:45); however, common grace is not enough to reconcile us to a holy God. For that, we need special, divine grace, or, in the words of

Peter, "the true grace of God." The true grace of God of which Peter wrote is that Christ suffered for our sins to give us his resurrection life and fellowship with God. His redeeming grace comes through faith in Christ, which is a gift (Eph. 2:8) that cannot be earned. This true grace, however, makes real claims on our lives. If we have truly encountered the free yet costly grace of God, we will persevere in trusting, obeying, adoring, repenting, and worshiping Jesus as Redeemer and King.

Whole-Bible Connections

SHEPHERD. Shepherd imagery stretches back to ancient Near Eastern cultures, in which shepherds were responsible for the protection and care of their flocks. Sometimes the idea of a shepherd was applied to kingly rule. In the Bible, shepherds are often held to account by God for their abuse and unsatisfactory care of God's people (Jeremiah 23; Zechariah 10–11; Jude 12). In their place, God promises better shepherds who will lead his people well. Psalm 23 reminds us that the archetypal Shepherd is God himself, who leads us beside still waters and restores our soul. In Christ, we discover the chief Shepherd, who succeeds where all other shepherds fail (1 Pet. 2:25; 5:4). Jesus goes through the valley of darkness to defeat sin, death, and evil in order to take his lambs into his arms and lead them into the green pastures of his love and a whole new creation (Isa. 40:11; John 10:1–18; Rev. 7:17).

Theological Soundings

ELDERS. Elders are responsible for the theological oversight and general shepherding of the church (Acts 20:17–35). Paul instructed the early church to appoint elders in every city to lead the churches there (Titus 1:5). Elders are accountable to God for their leadership and are to be men of godly character, an example to the flock (1 Tim. 3:1–7; Titus 1:5–9; 1 Pet. 5:3). Elders are also sometimes called pastors/shepherds or overseers (Eph. 4:11; Titus 1:5–7; Acts 20:17).

Personal Implications

Take time to reflect on the implications of 1 Peter 5:1–14 for your own life today. Consider what you have learned that might lead you to praise God, repent of sin, and trust in his promises. You can make notes below on the personal implications of the (1) *Gospel Glimpses*, (2) *Whole-Bible Connections*, (3) *Theological Soundings*, and (4) the passage as a whole.

1. Gospel Glimpses

2. Whole-Bible Connections

3. Theological Soundings

4. 1 Peter 5:1–14

> ## As You Finish This Unit . . .

Look back through this unit to reflect on some key things you have learned. Pause to celebrate God's grace, wisdom, and presence in your life.

Definition

[1] **Devil** – Scripture identifies the Devil as Satan, naming him the accuser (Zech. 3:1), the tempter (Matt. 4:3), and the deceiver (Rev. 12:9), and he is pictured in Revelation 12 as a dragon, by reason of his fierce hostility. While we should be clear-eyed and watchful for his temptations, the Devil was dealt a decisive blow in Jesus' death and resurrection (Gen. 3:15; Luke 10:18; Col. 2:13–15). Satan has been put on notice, having been bound in order to no longer deceive the nations (Rev. 20:2), but his influence is still present. God will overthrow him once for all when he is cast into the lake of fire (Rev. 20:10).

Week 7: God's Grace for a Life of Godliness

2 Peter 1:1–15

The Place of the Passage

A few years after penning 1 Peter, the apostle Peter writes to the same general audience (2 Pet. 3:1) and sounds many of the same themes. Two themes are intensified in 2 Peter—false teaching and eschatology[1]—as the apostle responds to heretical teaching that has arisen. Peter does not take up a lengthy apologetic against the various heresies but instead affirms and reaffirms the authority and inspiration of his own writing and that of other writers of Scripture. He views his own writings as affectionate reminders of God's truth and urges his readers to trust God's "precious and very great promises" (2 Pet. 1:4). Chapter 1 of the epistle generally focuses on knowing Christ, while chapter 2 homes in on the danger of denying Christ and chapter 3 focuses on the return of Christ.

Outline of 2 Peter

VI. The Grace of God for a Life of Godliness (1:1–15)

  A. Salutation (1:1–2)
  B. Divine grace for godliness (1:3–11)
  C. A stirring reminder (1:12–15)

VII. The Glory of Christ as the Basis for Scripture (1:16–21)

    A. Eyewitness testimony to Christ (1:16–18)

    B. The prophetic word confirmed (1:19–21)

VIII. The Judgment of False Teachers and Those Who Go Along with Them (2:1–22)

    A. A warning regarding false teachers (2:1–3)

    B. Judgment of false teachers (2:4–22)

IX. The Return of Jesus Is Certain (3:1–18)

    A. The timing and nature of the Lord's return (3:1–13)

    B. Life with an eye on the Lord's return (3:14–18)

The Big Picture

Second Peter 1:1–15 presents a strong call to godliness, enabled by God's power working through his Word.

Reflection and Discussion

Read through the complete passage for this study, 2 Peter 1:1–15. Then review the questions below concerning this opening section of 2 Peter and write your notes on them. (For further background, see the *ESV Study Bible*, pages 2418–2419; available online at esv.org.)

1. Salutation (1:1–2)

Peter opens the letter by referring to himself as "Simeon Peter"—Simeon is the Jewish spelling of the name Simon and is used only one other time in the New Testament (Acts 15:14). The use of this Jewish name underscores Peter's identity as the author of the letter. What other hints do you see in this opening section (vv. 1–15) that point to Peter as the author of this epistle?

Peter greets his audience as those who "have obtained a faith of equal standing with ours by the righteousness of our God and Savior Jesus Christ" (1:1). Read Romans 3:21–26 and consider the parallels between these two passages. Why do we have a standing before God equal to that of the apostles? Why does Peter include this in his greeting?

2. Divine Grace for Godliness (1:3–11)

The word "divine" appears twice in verses 3–4. What is Peter referring to with this term, and why does he repeat it? According to these verses, what is the basis and goal of the Christian life? How may we obtain this goal?

Verses 5–7 list qualities reminiscent of Jesus. List them, noting which are prevalent in your life and which are lacking. Take some time to praise God for what is present and reflect on why certain ones are absent. Where can you see the connection between your weaker qualities and being "ineffective or unfruitful in the knowledge of our Lord Jesus Christ" (1:8)?

Read 2 Peter 1:8; 2:20; 3:18. What is the goal of biblical knowledge?

Second Peter 1:10 calls us to be diligent in confirming our calling and election. Revisit 1 Peter 1 and locate similar statements there. What does it mean to "confirm your calling and election"? Why is this so critical?

3. A Stirring Reminder (1:12–15)

The word translated "stir . . . up" means to awaken or stimulate. Why is Peter writing a "reminder"? Why do we need it?

Read through the following three sections on *Gospel Glimpses*, *Whole-Bible Connections*, and *Theological Soundings*. Then take time to consider the *Personal Implications* these sections may have for you.

Gospel Glimpses

KNOWLEDGE OF CHRIST. Peter repeats the word "knowledge" throughout this letter (2 Pet. 1:2, 3, 8; 2:20; 3:18). We often associate knowledge with reason and intellect. While the Scriptures certainly value the life of the mind, Peter homes in on a particular kind of knowledge: "knowledge of him who called us" (1:3). Peter concludes his letter with a similar remark, calling us to "grow in the grace and knowledge of our Lord and Savior Jesus Christ" (3:18). Biblical knowledge is meant to be personal and intimate, focused on knowing Christ. Memorized verses, theological depth, and gospel sayings are not enough to avoid temptation and error or to grow in godliness. Such growth requires adoration of God. The invitation to increase in knowledge is paired with a promise of divine power to apprehend the majesty of Jesus. Let us avoid the temptation to rely on biblical knowledge alone and rejoice that God is disposed to move us toward a more intimate knowledge of Jesus.

Whole-Bible Connections

RIGHTEOUSNESS OF GOD. The "righteousness of God" can refer to God's justice, his moral character, or his saving activity. God's righteousness accords with his character and is the basis of his judgment and salvation. All people lack the moral righteousness of God and are in desperate need of his saving righteousness. Fortunately, God is both "just and the justifier" of those who have faith in Jesus (Rom. 3:26; see also Gen. 15:6; Rom. 3:21–26). He upholds his justice by punishing the guilty, and he forgives and justifies sinners through Jesus' vindicating death and resurrection in our place. Second Peter 1:1 likely blends these three aspects of God's righteousness as Peter states that his readers have a right standing with God through Christ, not through the false teachings of the heretics.

Theological Soundings

KINGDOM OF GOD. The kingdom of God is the realm in which God reigns through the rule of Jesus. This realm is focused on God's people and God's eventual new creation. Jesus frequently spoke of the "kingdom of heaven," an equivalent term, noting that it broke into this world through his ministry: "If it is by the finger of God that I cast out demons, then the kingdom of God has come upon you" (Luke 11:20). Yet, Peter states, "There will be richly provided for you an entrance into the eternal kingdom of our Lord and Savior Jesus Christ" (2 Pet. 1:11). The kingdom of God is therefore both present and future. It is present in Jesus' rule over his people and future in his promised return to subdue finally all of his enemies and to dwell among all of his people in his eternal new creation (2 Pet. 3:13).

Personal Implications

Take time to reflect on the implications of 2 Peter 1:1–15 for your own life today. Consider what you have learned that might lead you to praise God, repent of sin, and trust in his promises. You can make notes below on the personal implications of the (1) *Gospel Glimpses*, (2) *Whole-Bible Connections*, (3) *Theological Soundings*, and (4) the passage as a whole.

1. Gospel Glimpses

2. Whole-Bible Connections

3. Theological Soundings

4. 2 Peter 1:1–15

> ### As You Finish This Unit . . .

As you reflect on this unit, consider some key things God may want you to carry throughout your study. Pause to ask the Holy Spirit for help to respond as the Lord wants you to.

Definition

[1] **Eschatology** – Study of the events that will occur in the "last days," including a time of tribulation, the return of Christ, the resurrection of humanity, divine judgment, the casting into hell of unrepentant sinners, and the new creation. Eschatology, as the word is now used, also has to do with the reign of Christ breaking into this world, which began with the incarnation.

Week 8: The True Word and False Teachers

2 Peter 1:16–2:22

After assuring his readers of the divine grace that will empower them to live godly lives, Peter explains why they should trust apostolic[1] teaching over and against false teachers: it will give them greater conviction to live in a Christlike way and will establish a basis for debunking false teachings.

The Big Picture

In 2 Peter 1:16–2:22, Peter explains why the apostles' writings can be trusted over false teachers and also warns of the consequences of false teaching.

Reflection and Discussion

Read the entire text for this week's study, 2 Peter 1:16–2:22. Then review the following questions concerning this section of 2 Peter and write your notes on them. (For further background, see the *ESV Study Bible*, pages 2419–2422; available online at esv.org.)

1. Eyewitness Testimony to Christ (1:16–18)

Peter grounds his stirring reminder (1:1–15) not in clever philosophy or fanciful Greek tales but in the eyewitness testimony of Jesus, which Peter shared with other apostles. How does this set Christianity apart? Why does it lend credibility to apostolic writing? Consider what you look for when you want to learn more about an important event.

Read Matthew 17:1–8 alongside 2 Peter 1:16–18. When Peter mentions Jesus' "honor and glory" at the transfiguration, what particular elements of the event might he be referring to? What do these elements tell us about Jesus and his kingdom (see Matt. 16:28)?

2. Prophetic Word Confirmed (1:19–21)

In addition to being taught by the Son of God, Peter points to a second source of reliability: "We have the prophetic word more fully confirmed" (2 Pet. 1:19). The "prophetic word" is likely a broad reference to the Old Testament (see 2 Pet.

1:20; 3:16). The word "confirm" is also used in 2 Peter 1:10. With these things in view, what does it mean for the prophetic word to be "confirmed"?

In 2 Peter 1:19, Peter says that we would do well to pay attention to the prophetic word in a particular way. Read Numbers 24:17 and Romans 13:11–14. What role does light and darkness play in these verses? How do these texts illuminate the way in which we should pay attention to God's Word? How can you take steps to do so?

In 2 Peter 1:20–21, Peter gives a third reason for the reliability of his writing. What is it? This text explains the process of biblical inspiration.[2] Reflecting on this verse, explain *inspiration* in your own words.

3. Warning and Judging False Teachers (2:1–22)

With a firm sense of the reliability of apostolic writing, Peter turns his attention to false teachers. According to 2:1–3, what motivates these false teachers? What is their principal error?

In 2 Peter 2:4–8, Peter identifies two threads of judgment and salvation across four cases. Identify the cases associated with judgment and salvation. What makes them distinct?

The first example of judgment (v. 4) may refer to those evildoers mentioned in Genesis 6:1–2 and/or Jude 6. What is Peter's primary concern in highlighting the judgment of these fallen angels?

The second example of judgment refers to Genesis 18–19. According to 2 Peter 2:10 and Jude 8, what two sins were being judged in that episode? Compare your answer to the sins Paul reviews in Romans 1:18–25. Why are these sins mentioned in particular?

Read 2 Peter 2:9. What is Peter's main point in describing these episodes of salvation and judgment?

Who are the "glorious ones" in 2:10? Read Jude 8–10. What do those who blaspheme these glorious ones reveal about themselves?

Verses 12–16 elaborate on the just punishment of false teachers. What additional motivations does Peter say will be judged? How should Peter's decisive statements of judgment awaiting false teachers impact your view of sound versus false doctrine?

Read verses 20–22. Why is the "last state . . . worse than the first"? How does this shed light on the call to confirm one's own calling and election (2 Pet. 1:10)?

Read through the following three sections on *Gospel Glimpses*, *Whole-Bible Connections*, and *Theological Soundings*. Then take time to consider the *Personal Implications* these sections may have for you.

Gospel Glimpses

THE MAJESTY OF CHRIST. Peter declares that he and other apostles were eyewitnesses to the majesty of the Lord Jesus Christ (2 Pet. 1:16). Can you imagine being on the Mount of Transfiguration, witnessing the glory of Christ, so strong that it radiated from within him, turning his clothing bright white? The witnesses heard the voice of the Father, declaring, "This is my beloved Son, with whom I am well pleased" (Matt. 17:5). No other person in the pages of Scripture or in the course of world history has received this perfect approval. And yet, through our repentance from sin and our faith in Jesus, his majesty becomes our glory (Col. 1:27; Rom. 8:30; 1 John 3:2). His approval becomes ours; his status, ours. Surely this is grace and peace multiplied (2 Pet. 1:2)!

Whole-Bible Connections

HOLY MOUNTAIN. Mountains have been important to most world cultures throughout history. The primordial garden of Eden was on a mountain, littered with precious stones, filled with botanical life, and marked by life-giving rivers flowing through it (Genesis 2; Ezek. 28:11–19). The Sumerians and Babylonians built temples atop mountains, where the gods were said to visit. Moses encountered the Lord on Mount Sinai, where Moses received the Ten Commandments (Exodus 24). What do the mountains in the Bible have in common? The presence of transcendence. When Peter, James, and John witnessed the glory and honor of Jesus on a mountain, the setting trumpeted the truth that Jesus was not just a man from Nazareth but is also the transcendent Son of God. The Messiah destined to rule the world in righteousness and peace had come! The transfiguration provided a peek into the future, when people will stream to the mountain-temple of God and every knee will bow and every tongue confess that Jesus Christ is Lord (Isaiah 60; Phil. 2:10–11).

Theological Soundings

PERSEVERANCE OF THE SAINTS. Peter reminds his readers that "the Lord knows how to rescue the godly from trials" (2 Pet. 2:9)—the Lord will surely save to the end those whom he has called and justified. And yet the apostle urges his readers to "confirm" their calling and election (1:10). These twin truths emphasize what is sometimes called the "perseverance of the saints." Although we are justified by faith alone through grace alone, faith never remains alone. True faith makes much of grace. It is opposed to earning but not to working. Paul reminds us, "Work out your own salvation with fear and trembling" (Phil. 2:12), and Jesus says, "The one who endures to the end will be saved" (Matt. 24:13). Peter reminds us that we are to make every effort to add to our faith virtue (2 Pet. 1:5). Perseverance deepens our knowledge of Christ as we close in on his eternal kingdom (2 Pet. 1:11).

Personal Implications

Take time to reflect on the implications of 2 Peter 1:16–2:22 for your own life today. Consider what you have learned that might lead you to praise God, repent of sin, and trust in his promises. You can make notes below on the personal implications of the (1) *Gospel Glimpses*, (2) *Whole-Bible Connections*, (3) *Theological Soundings*, and (4) the passage as a whole.

1. Gospel Glimpses

2. Whole-Bible Connections

3. Theological Soundings

4. 2 Peter 1:16–2:22

As You Finish This Unit . . .

This unit has is a lot to take in. Take some time to look back through it and reflect on some key things the Lord may be teaching you.

Definitions

[1] **Apostolic** –That which pertains to the writing and ministry of the apostles of Jesus. An apostle was someone who was chosen and sent by Jesus to represent him.

[2] **Biblical inspiration** – The process of fallible men receiving God's infallible word and writing it down as Scripture. The term comes from 2 Timothy 3:16: "All Scripture is breathed out [inspired] by God."

Week 9: The Day of the Lord Is Coming

2 Peter 3:1–18

The Place of the Passage

In this final chapter, Peter focuses on one of the questions false teachers were raising: "Where is the promise of his coming?" (3:4). In responding to this false claim that there would be no judgment or return of Christ, Peter provides insight into what we can expect upon the Lord's return, as well as instruction in how we should live in the meantime. Peter concludes the letter by repeating themes mentioned in the letter's opening, such as the knowledge of God, perseverance in faith, and the reliability of the Scriptures.

The Big Picture

Second Peter 3:1–18 teaches that the return of the Lord is certain and that it should change the way we live now.

Reflection and Discussion

Read through the complete text for this study, 2 Peter 3:1–18. Then review the questions below concerning this part of 2 Peter and write your notes on them. (For further background, see the *ESV Study Bible*, pages 2422–2423; available online at esv.org.)

1. The Timing and Nature of the Lord's Return (3:1–13)

Verses 1–3 underscore the importance of being reminded of the prophetic word (contained in the Old Testament) and apostolic teaching (which became the New Testament). Yet Peter has already mentioned that his readers are "established in the truth that you have" (2 Pet. 1:12). If these Christians already know the truth, why is Peter reminding them of it?

Peter's reminder comes with a warning: "Scoffers will come in the last days" (3:3). When are the "last days"? Consider the following passages as you answer: Daniel 12:1–3; Matthew 24:4–9; Acts 2:17; Hebrews 1:2; Jude 12.

Why are the scoffers so dangerous? According to 2 Peter 3:4, what is their primary objection? How has Peter already combatted this view (consider 1 Pet. 1:3–5)?

How does Peter answer the scoffers' objection (2 Pet. 3:5–7)? If the universe was created out of nothing, why does Peter say God created the earth "out of water"? What is the relevance of a water-fashioned earth to his argument?

If God's "word" stands behind his use of water to create and destroy (2 Pet. 3:5–6), what bearing does this have on the claim that God (in the form of Christ) is not coming back?

Read Psalm 90:1–4 alongside 2 Peter 3:8. What is Peter teaching about God? About humanity?

According to verses 8–9, why does Christ delay his return? How does this compare to the attitude of the mockers?

In verse 10, Peter describes the day of the Lord as a time of cosmic destruction and renewal. List the three realms he mentions and note what will happen to each.

2. Life with an Eye on the Lord's Return (3:14–18)

If we have "equal standing" with the apostles through the righteousness of Jesus (1:1), why does Peter tell us to "be diligent to be found by [Christ] without spot or blemish" (3:14)? Compare Philippians 2:14–15 as you answer.

What does 2 Peter 3:16 tell us about Peter's view of Paul's writings? What does it tell us about the study of Scripture?

What would it look like for you to take the warnings in verse 17 to heart? How should Peter's description of his readers as "beloved" influence our response to these warnings?

Peter has emphasized the knowledge of God throughout the letter. Why does he close by adding that we should grow in the "grace and knowledge" of Jesus (3:18)? How can you do so in your local church?

Read through the following three sections on *Gospel Glimpses*, *Whole-Bible Connections*, and *Theological Soundings*. Then take time to consider the *Personal Implications* these sections may have for you.

Gospel Glimpses

THE LORD IS NOT SLOW. One of the issues raised in 2 Peter is the delay of the Lord's return. Peter responds by saying, "The Lord is not slow to fulfill his promise as some count slowness" (3:9). At Peter's time of writing, it had been only a few years since Jesus' ascension, yet today almost two thousand years have gone by, giving perhaps even more reason to doubt the return of Christ. Yet Peter's words tell us that God is not slow, as some count slowness. The background to this quote reveals the stark difference between the divine and the human experience of time. Psalm 90 tells us that God is "from everlasting to everlasting" and that our lives are but a breath. We should therefore "number our days" in order to live wisely, not doubting God's ways or living foolishly. His "slowness" should generate humility, not doubt or despair. In fact, what we perceive as slowness is actually the grace of God unfolding over time. Were he "fast," many souls would not come to repentance. Redemptive history would be truncated, and you and I would not taste the goodness of the Lord. Thank God for his "slowness" as he pours out the riches of his grace across cultures, around the world, and throughout time so that people from every tribe, tongue, and nation can enter his eternal kingdom (Rev. 7:9).

Whole-Bible Connections

NEW HEAVENS AND EARTH. Peter uses destructive language to describe the dissolution of heaven and earth (2 Pet. 3:10–12). Isaiah 60 and Revelation 21–22 seem almost to contradict Peter when they describe a renewed cosmos, centered on the city of God upon Mount Zion, where people stream in to bring God tribute. How do we reconcile Peter's picture of the heavens being "set on fire" with Scripture's promise of a renewed heavens and earth? If the earth were utterly destroyed, what would happen to mankind, and how could we bring tribute to God? Somehow God purifies the elements of the earth to reuse them in his renewal of all creation. He does not simply replace his good creation, no matter how ruined it is. His does not consider this world to be disposable, nor does he privilege the "spiritual" over the physical. When Peter refers to the earth and its works, he says that they will be "exposed" (3:10). This verb means to "find out," not to "destroy." Therefore we must conclude that there will be both continuity and discontinuity between the present and future heavens and earth. However, all will face judgment,[1] and thus all should seek Jesus and live. Those who hope in Jesus for salvation will see his righteous rule extend into the very fabric of creation, in a new heavens and earth where righteousness dwells (2 Pet. 3:13).

Theological Soundings

CREATION OUT OF NOTHING. Although Peter says the world was made out of water, he emphasizes God's creative word behind that water (2 Pet. 3:5–6). This supports the Genesis 1 account, in which God speaks creation into existence as the Spirit hovers over the waters of the deep. The idea that the universe was created out of nothing is rooted in Hebrews 11:3: "By faith we understand that the universe was created by the word of God, so that what is seen was not made out of things that are visible." It is important to acknowledge God's sovereign, creative will in speaking the universe into existence. Early church fathers emphasized God's creation out of nothing in response to claims that matter was eternal. Their concern was to show from the Bible that there was no rival to the triune Creator (God vs. matter), since he has existed in self-sufficient harmony from eternity past.

WHEN WILL CHRIST RETURN? Jesus exhorts us to be ready for his return (Matt. 24:44). Peter and Paul say that the return of Christ will be like "a thief in the night," something that will come suddenly (2 Pet. 3:10; 1 Thess. 5:2). Jesus promises, "Surely I am coming soon" (Rev. 22:20). These texts seem to imply that Christ could return at any moment. Yet Christ describes many "signs of the times" that will occur before he returns: intensified suffering and tribulation, the rise of false messiahs and prophets, and the gospel's being preached to all nations (Mark 13). It is possible that all of these signs have already been fulfilled. Some Christians certainly have endured intense suffering, sometimes at the hands of false messiahs, while the gospel has been preached in most of the world. Yet it is impossible to know the day or the hour of Christ's return. Therefore we should live as though his return is imminent, while being aware of how much gospel ministry remains to be done. Jesus' return should motivate anticipation, sobriety, hope, and holiness as we participate with his Spirit and pray for his kingdom to come and his will to be done, on earth as it is in heaven.

Personal Implications

Take time to reflect on the implications of 2 Peter 3:1–18 for your own life today. Consider what you have learned that might lead you to praise God, repent of sin, and trust in his promises. You can make notes below on the personal implications of the (1) *Gospel Glimpses*, (2) *Whole-Bible Connections*, (3) *Theological Soundings*, and (4) the passage as a whole.

1. Gospel Glimpses

2. Whole-Bible Connections

3. Theological Soundings

4. 2 Peter 3:1–18

As You Finish This Unit . . .

Take a moment to look back through this unit of study, to reflect on some key things that the Lord may be teaching you.

Definition

[1] **Judgment** – Any assessment of something or someone, especially moral assessment. The Bible also speaks of a final day of judgment when Christ returns, when all those who have refused to repent will be judged (Rev. 20:12–15).

WEEK 10: CONTENDING FOR THE FAITH

Jude 1–16

The Place of the Passage

The book of Jude bears many similarities to 2 Peter and likely predates that letter. Jude, the brother of Jesus, writes to Christians to warn them of those who pervert the grace of God, exhorting them to contend for the faith. He frequently alludes to Old Testament stories to illustrate God's judgment while also pointing to God's saving work in Christ. His use of vivid images reveals the futility of trying to escape God's authority.

The Big Picture

In Jude 1–16, Jude calls Christians to contend for the faith amid ungodly people who pervert God's grace.

▶ Reflection and Discussion

Read through the complete passage for this study, Jude 1–16. Then review the questions below on the first half of this letter and record your notes and reflections. (For further background, see the *ESV Study Bible*, pages 2449–2452; available online at esv.org.)

What is surprising about Jude's self-identification in 1:1?

In verse 1, the "called" are described as "beloved" and "kept," with those two descriptors occurring in a tense that implies something completed in the past but with ongoing effect. How might this understanding affect the way you interpret this verse? Why do you suppose Jude chose those specific words to open this letter?

The purpose of the letter is communicated in verse 3. What is it? Read Acts 6:7; Galatians 1:23; and Philippians 1:27 to determine the meaning of "the faith."

The word "contend" (Jude 3) comes from a military or athletic context and conveys a sense of "intense effort." Verses 20–23 detail how we are to contend for the faith. Describe what an intense effort would look like for you in these areas.

Verse 5 describes Jesus as the leader of the exodus and the destroyer of those who did not believe during that time. Read Numbers 14:1–38. Who are the destroyed unbelievers to whom Jude refers? How could *Jesus* have been the destroyer if Yahweh was the one who led Israel out of Egypt?

With the sovereignty of Jesus firmly established, Jude points to eight cases of rebellion in the following verses. Verses 5–7 include three groups: a generation of unbelieving Israelites, angels, and cities. Why were these groups punished?

Verse 7 condemns sexual immorality and those who "pursued unnatural desire." Read Genesis 19:1–11. What sin of Sodom is Jude referring to? What point is Jude making?

In verse 8, Jude returns to the false teachers and summarizes some of their faults. What are they? In verse 9 he recounts a Jewish story likely contained in a book called the *Assumption of Moses*.[1] Read Zechariah 3:1–5 for a similar story, which will help you interpret Jude's point. What is his point in telling this story (see Jude 10)?

Verse 11 strings three Old Testament accounts together: Cain (Genesis 4), Balaam (Numbers 22–24), and Korah (Numbers 16). What is the principal error in each case?

Notice that the false teachers often go undetected, like "hidden reefs at your love feasts" (Jude 12). How can churches be more discerning about such threats?

In verses 12–13 Jude piles up descriptors to indict the false teachers. Why is he so adamant about their fruitlessness and shame? What does he want to convey to the church, and how should this impact the way we contend for the faith?

In verses 14–15 Jude quotes from *1 Enoch*[2] to illustrate God's judgment against the "ungodly" teachers (Jude 15; see also v. 4). Why is "ungodly" an apt description?

_____

_____

_____

_____

_____

_____

Verse 16 summarizes the faults of the false teachers. Can you distill their errors under two headings? In contrast, how does God extend true advantage to us (vv. 1–2)?

_____

_____

_____

_____

_____

Read through the following three sections on *Gospel Glimpses*, *Whole-Bible Connections*, and *Theological Soundings*. Then take time to consider the *Personal Implications* these sections may have for you.

Gospel Glimpses

KEPT FOR JESUS. Jude repeats the word "kept" throughout his letter. Rebellious angels do not "keep" their place of authority but instead trade it out for lesser things (v. 6). As a result, they are "kept" in chains for the day of judgment. Similarly, the gloom of utter darkness is "kept" for the false teachers. These failures serve as warnings to us, which is why Jude exhorts Christians to "keep" themselves in the love of God (v. 21). Doing so will lead to a much brighter future, one populated with eternal life and with greater joy in the meantime. However, all of us at times wander from the love of God. While it is certainly our responsibility to endure in the faith and seek the embrace of our loving heavenly Father, it is ultimately God's sovereign grace that "keeps" us in his love. After all, we are "beloved in God the Father and kept for Jesus Christ" (v. 1). God's keeping precedes and empowers our keeping; it is his sturdy embrace and electing love that satisfy the soul, and we must train our souls to pant after his perfect love.

Whole-Bible Connections

THE EXODUS. In Exodus 19:4, the Lord clearly takes credit for the exodus rescue of Israel: "You yourselves have seen what I did to the Egyptians, and how I bore you on eagles' wings and brought you to myself." The exodus is the defining event for the Old Testament people of God, as God rescued his people from slavery and constituted them as his chosen nation. On the Mount of Transfiguration, Moses and Elijah refer to Jesus' upcoming "departure" (Gk. *exodon*) in Jerusalem, where he would be crucified and then raised from the dead (Luke 9:31). This exodus language refocuses the reader's attention onto Jesus as a second Moses figure whose leadership, suffering, and resurrection would accomplish a permanent rescue for the people of God. By assigning Jesus the very role claimed by Yahweh himself (Jude 5), Jude shows that Jesus is Yahweh—he is truly God.

Theological Soundings

DOUBLE PREDESTINATION. Jude mentions people "who long ago were designated for this condemnation" (v. 4). The idea that some are predestined for salvation and others for condemnation can be difficult to swallow. Some prefer to emphasize the freedom of human choice. However, if we were truly "brought forth in iniquity," and "in sin did [our] mother conceive [us]" (Ps. 51:5), then our will is able only to dishonor God and is thus unable to choose Christ. An unregenerate heart, then, is cold to the beauty and lordship of Jesus and cannot willingly glorify God. This is not to diminish moral choices, for Scripture recognizes that good choices are possible regardless of one's position before God (Matt. 7:9–10; Rom. 13:3). Yet all our choices are ultimately good or bad because they come from a good or bad heart (Matt. 7:15–19). Therefore all are condemned apart from the intervention of God's saving grace. God has chosen vessels of mercy alongside vessels of wrath, both of which have been prepared beforehand for his glory (Rom. 9:22–23). Vessels of wrath glorify God's righteous justice in punishing evil, while vessels of mercy magnify God's mercy in saving repentant sinners. We have no right to grace; Jesus unilaterally secures grace for his people. Double predestination, then, refers to God's sovereign freedom to appoint some to salvation and others to condemnation.

HOMOSEXUALITY. Sodom and Gomorrah are often offered as examples of divine judgment on homosexuality. Jude compares the exploits of angels in verse 6 to sexual immorality in verse 7. Just as a boundary was transgressed by angels who sought relations with humans (see Gen. 6:1–2), so was a boundary transgressed by the men in Sodom. In Jude 7, the phrase translated "pursued unnatural desire" literally means "pursued other flesh." Some commentators have argued that this refers to the men of Sodom's pursuit of angelic flesh; however, there was no way for them at first to know the men were angels. The narrative clearly indicates that they desired to "know" the angels, an idiom frequently used to describe sexual relations (Gen. 19:8); Lot responds by condemning their actions as "wicked" (Gen. 19:7). It is thus likely that homosexual intercourse is in view, though the forceful demands of the crowd also indicate something like rape. Jude clearly describes this action as sexually immoral (Jude 7). Nevertheless, Scripture does reveal another reason for God's judgment on Sodom: In a passage that also condemns the "abomination" of Sodom's sin (Ezek. 16:47, 50; Lev. 20:13), the prophet Ezekiel further declares, "Behold, this was the guilt of your sister Sodom: she and her daughters had pride, excess of food, and prosperous ease, but did not aid the poor and needy" (Ezek. 16:49). In the end, God judged these cities not for a single sin but for a whole mountain of rebellious sins. Therefore, we should not elevate homosexual sin above others; Paul includes it as one sin among other serious sins (1 Cor. 6:9; 1 Tim. 1:10), even while recognizing it as an egregious example of rebellion against God, and of his judgment of such rebellion (Rom. 1:24–27). We should extend the promise of forgiveness to all who repent and put their faith in Christ, while recognizing that homosexual sin, like any sin, may require time to break free from totally (1 Cor. 6:11).

Personal Implications

Take time to reflect on the implications of Jude 1–16 for your own life today. Consider what you have learned that might lead you to praise God, repent of sin, and trust in his promises. You can make notes below on the personal implications of the (1) *Gospel Glimpses*, (2) *Whole-Bible Connections*, (3) *Theological Soundings*, and (4) the passage as a whole.

1. Gospel Glimpses

2. Whole-Bible Connections

3. Theological Soundings

4. Jude 1–16

As You Finish This Unit . . .

Take a moment to look back through this unit of study and to reflect on some key things that the Lord may be teaching you.

Definitions

[1] *Assumption of Moses* –An uninspired pseudepigraphal book (a book whose real author is unknown) containing Jewish history and theology, probably written around the time of Jesus. A few phrases and sentences from this book appear in Scripture: see Jude 9, 16, 18.

[2] *1 Enoch* – A diverse, uninspired pseudepigraphal book that includes helpful information regarding the history, theology, and eschatology of Judaism, written over an extended period of time by various authors.

WEEK 11: PERSEVERING IN THE FAITH

Jude 17–25

▲

The Place of the Passage

After addressing the follies and judgment of false teachers, Jude turns his attention to how believers can contend for the faith. His instruction culminates in one of the best-known doxologies of the New Testament (Jude 24–25). Clearly understanding verses 1–23 increases the potency of this magnificent doxology.

The Big Picture

Jude implores us to heed his warnings, persevere in the faith, and extend the mercy of God to others as eternity draws nearer.

> ## Reflection and Discussion

Read through Jude 17–25, the passage for this week's study. Then review the following questions, taking notes on the final portions of this letter. (For further background, see the *ESV Study Bible*, pages 2451–2452; available online at esv.org.)

What is it that is so important for believers to remember, according to verse 17 (see 2 Pet. 3:1–3)? Read Acts 20:29–30 for an example.

Picking up on his charge to "contend for the faith" (v. 3), Jude aims to steer the church away from self-made moralities and an anti-authoritarian streak (vv. 18–19), which pervert the grace of God. How do you "contend for the faith" when faced with moral positions that do not align with Scripture?

Using "but" in verse 20, Jude contrasts the beloved with the scoffers. If scoffers are worldly people who cause divisions and are devoid of the Spirit (vv. 18–19), what should believers look like (vv. 20–23)?

Reflect on what befell those who did not keep themselves in the love of God (vv. 5–13). What would it look like for you to better keep yourself in the love of God? What does the repetition of "yourselves" imply (vv. 20–21)?

In verse 21 Jude says that one way we keep ourselves in the love of God is by "waiting for the mercy of our Lord Jesus Christ." But in verse 2 he prays for mercy to be "multiplied" to us. The word "waiting" (v. 21) means "to look forward to" (Mark 15:43; Titus 2:13). How do we *receive* mercy and *wait for* mercy at the same time?

In verse 22, Jude turns our attention to how we should respond to those around us. First, he tells us to "have mercy on those who doubt." The word for "doubt" indicates someone who asks questions. How should your responses to a scoffer and a doubter differ?

Next, Jude says we ought to save others by "snatching them out of the fire[1]" (v. 23). This implies that this second group of people is in great danger. When the threat of fire is upon you, how do you respond? What should "snatching" others look like in your relationships?

A final category of people includes those who have been stained by their sins. What is to be hated in this verse? Who is to be shown mercy? Why does Jude say to do this in "fear"? How should Jesus' teaching in Matthew 18:15–17 influence this?

Verses 24–25 function not as an afterword but as a climax to the whole letter. How do they do so?

The first half of this doxology[2] (v. 24) emphasizes what God does for us, while the second half (v. 25) emphasizes who God is. How do the two interrelate?

How does one stand and not fall in the presence of the only God to whom belong glory, majesty, dominion, and authority?

Read through the following three sections on *Gospel Glimpses*, *Whole-Bible Connections*, and *Theological Soundings*. Then take time to consider the *Personal Implications* these sections may have for you.

Gospel Glimpses

MOST HOLY FAITH. Paul exhorts the Philippians to live in a "manner worthy of the gospel" and to strive "side by side for the faith of the gospel" (Phil. 1:27). The gospel is a gospel that calls for faith, and thus "the faith" can serve as shorthand for that gospel (see Acts 6:7). By describing it as "most holy" (Jude 20), Jude sets "the faith" apart from the false and unholy teachings peddled by scoffers and ungodly teachers. The "most holy faith" is distinct from all other teachings because it is the eternal gospel revealed from heaven (Rev. 14:6); it centers on the person of Jesus Christ and his unique work of reconciling sinful humanity to a holy God, to the praise of his glorious grace (Ephesians 1).

THE LOVE OF GOD. Jude opens and closes his letter by describing Christians as "beloved" (vv. 1, 17). This indicates that Christians do not merely receive the benefit of the occasional love of God; rather, they possess an identity as the very beloved children of God (1 John 3:1). This love is not shaped by our good nature, fine doctrine, church affiliation, great character, or good works; it is the unearned, freely bestowed affection of the Father, through the Son, despite our sinfulness—affection that is poured out lavishly into our hearts by the Spirit (Rom. 5:5; 8:37–39). Nothing can separate us from the love of God in Christ Jesus.

Whole-Bible Connections

ETERNAL LIFE. Jude closes his letter by exhorting Christians to keep their eyes on the mercy of the Lord Jesus that leads to eternal life (v. 21). Adam and Eve enjoyed the possibility of eternal life (Gen. 3:22) as they enjoyed actual fellowship with God, but it was compromised by their rebellion against him. The possibility of eternal life returns to humanity through faith in Jesus and the work of the Spirit (Titus 3:5–7). This life includes the promise of resurrection bodies, which will no longer be encumbered by the corruption of sin (1 Corinthians 15). Eternal life is also quantitative, lasting forever, as the word clearly conveys. Above all, Jesus Christ is our eternal life (John 17:3), and his return will suffuse heaven and earth and all the saints with his glorious, renewing power and grace. This state of bodily and spiritually whole existence will last forever in God's unfading and unending new creation (1 Pet. 1:3–5). Eternal life, then, is not merely an infinite lifespan in a cloudy heaven, but the promise of an embodied, forever existence unhindered by sin, death, and evil in a renewed cosmos. Surely this reward should motivate worship, perseverance, mercy, and evangelism, all to the glory of God.

Theological Soundings

ETERNAL FIRE. Jude states that the teachers who subvert God's authority and indulge in sexual immorality will undergo a punishment of eternal fire (v. 7). Jesus uses the same language to describe the fate of the wicked (Matt. 18:8; 25:41). There is some debate as to the eternality of this eternal fire. Some scholars argue that this is a metaphor for judgment and that the wicked will not endure eternal, conscious punishment. Consider Revelation 21:6–8: "As for the cowardly, the faithless, the detestable, as for murderers, the sexually immoral, sorcerers, idolaters, and all liars, their portion will be in the lake that burns with fire and sulfur, which is the second death." Commentators argue that this is a case of hyperbole, since water does not burn. Therefore, they contend, the fiery punishment must be figurative and limited. However, it is preferable to read the text plainly as describing a punishment that will last forever. Jude's comment is made in the context of the fiery destruction of Sodom and Gomorrah, a literal yet temporary event that serves as an "eternal" reminder of the coming eternal fire. The emphasis on smoke curling up forever in Revelation seems to contradict the temporary view of an eternal fire: "The smoke of their torment goes up forever and ever, and they have no rest, day or night" (Rev. 14:11). The punishment for rejecting God's gracious offer in Christ will be worse than anything we can imagine, and it will last forever. This should motivate gospel witness and an eager desire to help people persevere in the faith. On a hopeful note, the corollary will also be true of heaven—the reward of trusting in Christ will be better than anything we can imagine and will last for all eternity (Revelation 21–22).

DOUBT. Jude makes a distinction between scoffers and doubters. Scoffers are ill-motivated, immoral, and seek to undermine the authority of God for personal gain (financial, moral, relational, etc.) They mock the truth. Doubters, on the other hand, question the truth. They wrestle with big questions, difficult truths, and strange teachings. Such wrestling should not be condemned, and neither should the doubter. Even Jesus did not condemn Thomas when he doubted that Jesus has risen from the dead (John 20:24–29). Rather, Jesus gave him visible proof (scars) and reasoned with him (ghosts cannot eat fish). Similarly, we should show mercy on those who doubt and listen patiently to their questions, recognizing that a faith unquestioned or untested is of little value (1 Peter 1; James 1).

Personal Implications

Take time to reflect on the implications of Jude 17–25 for your own life today. Consider what you have learned that might lead you to praise God, repent of sin, and trust in his promises. You can make notes below on the personal implications of the (1) *Gospel Glimpses*, (2) *Whole-Bible Connections*, (3) *Theological Soundings*, and (4) the passage as a whole.

1. Gospel Glimpses

2. Whole-Bible Connections

3. Theological Soundings

4. Jude 17–25

▶ As You Finish This Unit . . .

Take a moment now to ask for the Lord's blessing and help as you continue in this study of Jude. And take a moment also to look back through this unit of study, to reflect on some key things that the Lord may be teaching you.

Definitions

[1] **Fire** – The imagery of fire is typically associated with divine punishment for unrepentant sinners and angels (Jude 7; Rev. 19:20), although it can also be used as an image for purification (1 Pet. 1:7; 1 Cor. 3:13–15).

[2] **Doxology** – Literally, "a word or saying of glory." A doxology is typically a compact reflection of the nature and work of God.

Week 12: Summary
and Conclusion

We conclude our study of 1–2 Peter and Jude by summarizing the big picture of God's message through these letters as a whole. Then we will consider several questions in order to reflect on various Gospel Glimpses, Whole-Bible Connections, and Theological Soundings throughout the entire book.

The Big Picture of 1 Peter, 2 Peter, and Jude

First Peter tells us that, no matter how dark or difficult the times, we have every reason to hope in Christ. This hope springs not from wishful thinking but from new life in Christ and his promised return, plus specific promises that he and the Father have given us. This new birth puts us on a trajectory toward a new heaven and earth, where Jesus will make all things right, good, and true. Peter proceeds to show how this hope in the return of Christ promotes perseverance, holiness, respect for authority, gospel witness, and humility in life lived together.

If 1 Peter explains a life lived in the hope of Christ's return, then 2 Peter responds to those who mock the idea of Jesus' return and final judgment. In contrast to those who peddle self-made philosophies and moralities, Peter calls Christians to an intimate knowledge of Christ grounded in God's holy Word. Summoning Old Testament stories for support, Peter demonstrates the Lord's pattern of rescuing the godly and punishing the wicked. Ultimate rescue and punishment are coming, and they are coming with Christ. Christians are not to be deceived but must be diligent, continuing to grow in the grace and knowledge of Jesus.

The epistle of Jude presses the church, in light of Christ's imminent return, to contend for the faith in times of controversy and chaos. Eager to maintain the purity of the gospel, Jude addresses destructive heresies that reject God's authority and goodness by promoting the authority of self and sinful pursuits. He, too, draws on Old Testament stories to serve as sure examples of God's coming judgment in Christ. Jude urges his readers to keep themselves in the love of God by building one another up, praying in the Spirit, and longing for the mercy of God at the return of Jesus Christ.

Gospel Glimpses

We have seen clear affirmations of the gospel of grace and the judgment of God in the person, work, and return of Jesus throughout 1–2 Peter and Jude. Have these letters brought new clarity to your understanding of the gospel? How so?

Were there any particular passages or themes that provoked fresh awe of Jesus?

Whole-Bible Connections

These letters are rich in whole-Bible stories, themes, and lessons. How has this study filled out your understanding of the biblical storyline of redemption?

Are there any particular themes in these letters that helped you better grasp the Bible's unity?

Have any passages or themes expanded your understanding of who God is, what he is doing in the world, and the relevance of Jesus' promised return?

What connections between these letters and the Old Testament were new to you?

Theological Soundings

Although often neglected, 1–2 Peter and Jude enrich and round out some significant Christian doctrines. Reflect on the doctrinal themes we have seen throughout these three letters. Has your own understanding of biblical theology been refined during the course of this study? How so?

How has your understanding of the nature and character of God been deepened throughout this study?

_____

_____

_____

_____

_____

What unique contributions do these letters make toward our understanding of who Jesus is and what he accomplished through his life, death, and resurrection?

_____

_____

_____

_____

_____

What specifically do these letters teach us about the human condition and our need of redemption?

_____

_____

_____

_____

_____

Personal Implications

God gave us these letters, ultimately, to help us endure in the faith, contend for the faith, and adore the object of our faith. It is important that these letters strengthen our communion with God, our gospel witness, and our personal character. As you reflect on the overall impact of these letters, what implications stand out for you?

_____

_____

_____

_____

_____

What stands out in general in your reflections on the Gospel Glimpses, Whole-Bible Connections, and Theological Soundings found in this study?

What in these letters has led you to praise God, turn away from sin, and trust more firmly in his promises?

▶ As You Finish Studying 1–2 Peter and Jude . . .

We rejoice with you as you finish studying the letters of 1–2 Peter and Jude! May this study become part of your Christian walk of faith, day by day and week by week throughout all your life. Now we encourage you to continue to study, apply, and share the Word of God. To help you as you continue your study of the Bible, you might consider other books in the *Knowing the Bible* series, or visit knowingthebibleseries.org.

Finally, take a moment to look back through this study. Review the notes that you have written and the things that you have highlighted or underlined. Reflect again on the key themes that the Lord has been teaching you. We pray that these truths and lessons will become a treasure for the rest of your life, in the name of the Father, and the Son, and the Holy Spirit. Amen.

KNOWING THE BIBLE STUDY GUIDE SERIES

Experience the *Grace* of God in the *Word* of God, Book by Book

Series Volumes

- Genesis
- Exodus
- Leviticus
- Numbers
- Deuteronomy
- Joshua
- Judges
- Ruth and Esther
- 1–2 Samuel
- 1–2 Kings
- 1–2 Chronicles
- Ezra and Nehemiah
- Job
- Psalms
- Proverbs
- Ecclesiastes
- Song of Solomon

- Isaiah
- Jeremiah
- Lamentations, Habakkuk, and Zephaniah
- Ezekiel
- Daniel
- Hosea
- Joel, Amos, and Obadiah
- Jonah, Micah, and Nahum
- Haggai, Zechariah, and Malachi
- Matthew
- Mark
- Luke

- John
- Acts
- Romans
- 1 Corinthians
- 2 Corinthians
- Galatians
- Ephesians
- Philippians
- Colossians and Philemon
- 1–2 Thessalonians
- 1–2 Timothy and Titus
- Hebrews
- James
- 1–2 Peter and Jude
- 1–3 John
- Revelation

crossway.org/knowingthebible